INDISSOLUBILITY AND THE SYNOD OF BISHOPS

Indissolubility
and the
Synod of Bishops

Reflections of a Canon Lawyer

John A. Alesandro, JCD, JD

Paulist Press
New York / Mahwah, NJ

Library of Congress Cataloging-in-Publication Data

Alesandro, John A., author.
    Indissolubility and the Synod of Bishops : reflections of a canon lawyer / John A. Alesandro, JCD, JD.
        pages cm
    ISBN 978-0-8091-4958-2 (pbk.) — ISBN 978-1-58768-562-0 (e-book)
    1. Marriage (Canon law) 2. Marriage—Annulment (Canon law) 3. Catholic Church. Synodus Episcoporum. 4. Councils and synods (Canon law) I. Title.
    KBR3155.A74 2015
    261.8'3581—dc23

                                                                                    2015010698

ISBN 978-0-8091-4958-2 (paperback)
ISBN 978-1-58768-562-0 (e-book)

Published by Paulist Press
997 Macarthur Boulevard
Mahwah, New Jersey 07430

www.paulistpress.com

Printed and bound in the
United States of America

Contents

Introduction

The convocation of the two Assemblies of the Synod of Bishops on "The Pastoral Challenges of the Family in the Context of Evangelization" engendered intense interest in the Church's teaching on marriage and family. At the outset, the extensive *instrumentum laboris* covered innumerable pastoral questions, touching on the Church's teaching on the family in Scripture and the Magisterium; the concept of natural law and its reception in the modern world; various pastoral programs for individuals, couples, and families; openness to life; and many other areas of pastoral concern.

In Part II of the document, The Pastoral Program for the Family in Light of New Challenges, the third chapter, which listed various difficult pastoral situations, alluded to couples who find themselves in marriages that are canonically irregular (§§89–92).[1] The document's pastoral approach stressed in particular the desire of such Catholics to receive holy communion (§§93–95) and the need to care for those who are divorced and remarried (§97). Paragraph 96, citing Pope Benedict XVI, alluded briefly to the interrelationship of faith and the sacrament of matrimony and also referenced the practice of the Orthodox in regard to second marriages. Finally, paragraphs 98–102 noted the call by various episcopal conferences to streamline the canonical process for declaring marriages invalid.

These reflections focus on a crucial area of the Synod's work: canonically irregular marriages, the principles implicated in the

Church's teaching on indissolubility, and the ways that canonical practice might be streamlined. We will divide the treatment of these issues as follows:

Part One: Sacramental and Indissoluble Marriage examines the underlying theological and canonical principles on which pastoral practice is based, the substantive teaching and law on marriage:

- A. *Anticipation of the Synod: Conflicting Views.* Well before the Third Extraordinary General Assembly of October 2014, voices were raised staking out differing positions about indissolubility, changes in pastoral practice and canonical process.
- B. *The Synod's Deliberations (October 5–19, 2014).* The pre-Synod conflicting views emerged in the Synod sessions themselves, leading to certain tentative conclusions for study, reflection, and treatment in greater depth in the October 2015 assembly.
- C. *Divorce and Remarriage.* The relatively late emergence of widespread divorce and remarriage has put considerable pressure on the Church's traditional "canonical construct" to govern pastoral decisions about marriage, divorce, and remarriage.
- D. *Indissolubility and Sacramentality.* The scriptural and theological basis for the indissolubility of sacramental marriages developed in a historical context. The principles that applied the teaching of Christ are in need of serious updating and renewal.
- E. *Consummation.* The historical development of the notion of consummation as an element of the indissolubility of marriage suggests a more flexible way of understanding the process by which sacramental marriages

become indissoluble. This approach could allow the Church to conclude, in certain pastoral situations, that individual sacramental marriages, if not invalid, may be shown by hindsight to be dissoluble.

Part Two: Streamlining Canon Law moves from the renewal of the sacramental meaning of marriage to the current canonical process for addressing irregular marriages as found in the Latin Code of Canon Law and how it can be updated.

A. *Substantive Marriage Law.* The revision of six areas of the Code would remove theological and canonical positions from the canons that hinder theological and pastoral development.

B. *Procedural Marriage Law.* There should be a complete revamping of the process the Church uses to address marriages that have ended in divorce and the irregular marriages that occur when divorced persons remarry civilly. We will suggest, as a start, the revision of eleven areas of canonical process.

Conclusions to the article offer a few final reflections on the need to rediscover the newness Christ brought to marriage and to update the Church's canonical implementation of Christ's teaching in this crucial area for Church order and discipline.

NOTE

1. Synod Secretariat, "The Pastoral Challenges of the Family in the Context of Evangelization: *Instrumentum Laboris* 2014," pars. 89–92, *Origins* 44, no. 10 (July 17, 2014): 172–73.

Part One:
Sacramental and
Indissoluble Marriage

A. ANTICIPATION OF THE SYNOD: CONFLICTING VIEWS

Prior to the Synod, various voices offered differing viewpoints on the most effective pastoral approach for the Church in the area of marriage. Some highlighted the plight of Catholics who, oftentimes with no real malice on their part, find themselves divorced and remarried in a union that the Church does not recognize as valid, because of which they are officially barred from receiving holy communion. Some, relying on the practice of *economia* of the Eastern Orthodox Churches, suggested a penitential pastoral practice which, while not permitting second irregular unions to be celebrated with the Church's blessing, nonetheless would permit such Christians to receive communion. Others saw any such accommodation as an aberration from Church teaching and practice and a not-so-subtle attack on the Church's teaching on the sacramentality and indissolubility of Christian marriage.

CARDINAL WALTER KASPER

One who, early on, raised for discussion the pastoral solution to such difficulties was Cardinal Walter Kasper at the extraordinary consistory of cardinals on February 20, 2014, who clarified at the outset his stance in regard to indissolubility:

> The indissolubility of sacramental marriage and the impossibility of a new marriage during the lifetime of the other partner is part of the tradition of the Church's binding faith that cannot be abandoned or undone by appealing to a superficial understanding of cheapened mercy. […] The question is therefore how the Church can reflect this indivisible pairing of the fidelity and mercy of God in its pastoral action concerning the divorced who are remarried in a civil ceremony.[1]

Kasper reiterated this stance in an article in the September 15, 2014 issue of *America*, titled "The Message of Mercy": "No theologian, not even the pope, can change the doctrine of the indissolubility of a sacramental marriage….But doctrine must be applied with prudence in a just and equitable way to concrete and often complex situations."[2]

In his February 2014 address at the consistory, Kasper distinguished two situations of the divorced and remarried in which he saw the possible development of a pastoral approach:

1. Those who "are in conscience subjectively convinced that their irreparably broken previous marriage was never valid," suggesting that the judicial resolution of such matters could perhaps be handled by "other more pastoral and spiritual procedures."

2. The "more difficult question of the situation of the marriage that is ratified and consummated between baptized persons, in which the communion of marital life is irreparably broken and one or both of the spouses have contracted a second civil marriage." Citing early Church practice, Kasper asks, "This way that stands beyond rigorism and laxity, the way of conversion, which issues forth in the sacrament of mercy, the sacrament of penance, is it also the path that we could follow in the present question?"

Differentiating his position from that of the Eastern Orthodox Churches who went on to admit other reasons for divorce besides adultery, Kasper noted,

The Western Church followed another path. It excludes the dissolution of a ratified and consummated sacramental marriage between baptized persons, but it acknowledges divorce for non-consummated marriage, as also, according to the Pauline and Petrine privilege, for non-sacramental marriages. Along with this are declarations of nullity for defect of form; in this regard we could however ask ourselves if what are brought to the forefront, in a unilateral way, are not juridical points of view that are historically very much late in coming.[3]

He questioned whether the Church would not be wise to return to the approach of the early fathers, like Basil the Great: "There can be no doubt however about the fact that in the early Church, in many local Churches, by customary law there was, after a time of repentance, the practice of pastoral tolerance, of clemency and indulgence."

Forty years ago, at the 1975 annual meeting of the Canon Law Society of America, Richard McCormick, SJ, raised a similar idea.

In his address on "Indissolubility and the Right to the Eucharist: Separate Issues or One?" McCormick analyzed the question and suggested that the indissolubility of a first marriage might be viewed more properly as a *moral* obligation, which could admit of repentance and absolution in individual cases if the first marriage were truly "dead." With this view, the second marriage, while not sacramental, would still be valid, and the spouses could receive communion. This suggestion was contrasted by McCormick to the traditional view that the indissoluble bond of the first marriage is a *doctrinal* bar to the validity of any remarriage and therefore, bars the spouses of the second union from communion unless, precluding all scandal, they live as brother-sister.[4]

CARDINAL GERHARD LUDWIG MÜLLER

Kasper's proposal for reflection and discussion caused quite a stir and some forceful push back. Archbishop (later Cardinal) Gerhard Ludwig Müller, Prefect of the CDF, had laid out an argument the previous October against such a change in pastoral practice.

Müller had provided a lucid exposition of the traditional magisterial teaching on the indissolubility of marriage. His reasoning included the following points:[5]

- Indissolubility is firmly grounded in the sacramentality of the marriage covenant. "Through the sacrament the indissolubility of marriage acquires a new and deeper sense: it becomes the image of God's enduring love for his people and of Christ's irrevocable fidelity to his Church."
- The "ideal of monogamy, but also that of indissolubility" is found in the Old Testament prophets' connection of marriage with the fidelity of God to his covenant with Israel.

- The principal locus of indissolubility in the New Testament is Jesus' debate with the Pharisees: the "Catholic Church has always based its doctrine and practice upon these sayings of Jesus concerning the indissolubility of marriage....It designates a reality that comes from God and is therefore no longer at man's disposal."
- Based on the disposition of 1 Corinthians 7:10–11, marriages between a baptized and unbaptized person can be dissolved by the "Pauline privilege" or the "favor of the faith." Such marriages are not "a sacrament in the true sense" and are not therefore marked by "unconditional indissolubility."
- Citing *Familiaris Consortio* 84, he states that the Church cannot adopt the Orthodox position and permit the invalidly remarried to receive communion: "Their state and condition of life objectively contradict that union of love between Christ and the Church which is signified and effected by the Eucharist" and "if these people were admitted to the Eucharist, the faithful would be led into error and confusion regarding the Church's teaching about the indissolubility of marriage."
- Because of today's culture, "marriages nowadays are probably invalid more often than they were previously, because there is a lack of desire for marriage in accordance with Catholic teaching, and there is too little socialization within an environment of faith."
- Müller does not allude to the Church's practice of dissolving the bond of sacramental marriages that are not physically consummated.

DOMINICAN THEOLOGIANS

A specific reaction to Cardinal Kasper's speech of February 20, 2014, was articulated by a group of Dominican theologians, rejecting the idea that the Church could permit invalidly remarried persons to receive holy communion. Their reasoning included the following points:[6]

- "Between two baptized persons, natural marriage cannot be separated from sacramental marriage."
- "A ratified and consummated marriage between two baptized persons cannot be dissolved by any human power, including the vicarious power of the Roman Pontiff."
- Marriage is essentially public.
- The Church should not abandon its insistence on the virtue of chastity for every person in accordance with their proper circumstances.
- Adopting the Eastern Orthodox practice of readmission to communion, "would inevitably require the Catholic Church to recognize and bless second marriages after divorce, which is clearly contrary to settled Catholic dogma and Christ's express teaching."
- Accepting divorced and remarried Catholics to communion "even as a 'merely' pastoral practice—requires that the Church accept in principle that sexual activity outside of a permanent and faithful marriage is compatible with communion with Christ and with the Christian life."
- In these cases, "spiritual communion" (as suggested for the divorced and remarried by Pope Benedict XVI) differs essentially from sacramental communion insofar as it represents "the desire for communion of a person conscious of grave sin or living in a situation that objectively contradicts

the moral law, who does not yet have a perfect communion with Christ in faith and charity."

- Forgiveness is impossible without repentance and firm purpose of amendment.
- A couple who "marries in the Church without an authentic commitment to the Church's faith or without an understanding of marriage's sacramental dimension" marries validly provided that they posit "valid consent according to the Catholic form." Such baptized persons might "not benefit from the graced *effects* of the sacrament, but *the sacrament itself is valid*…a valid marriage requires only that a person intend the natural goods of marriage."
- Annulments cannot be granted absent canonical expertise and procedures. "Subjective or personalized judgments in marriage cases" are "impossible."
- Their conclusion: "The Church's teaching on marriage, divorce, human sexuality, and chastity can be hard to receive. Christ himself saw this when he proclaimed it. However, this truth brings with it an authentic message of freedom and hope: there is a way out of vice and sin. There is a way forward that leads to happiness and love."

B. THE SYNOD'S DELIBERATIONS (OCTOBER 5–19, 2014)

At the outset, Pope Francis "called upon the Synod of Bishops to reflect upon the critical and invaluable reality of the family, a reflection which will then be pursued in greater depth at its Ordinary General Assembly scheduled to take place in October, 2015, as well as during the full year between the two synodal events."[7] Upon completion of the October 2014 sessions, a Synod Report (*Relatio Synodi*) was composed to summarize the deliberations and, in a concrete way, to prepare for a more in-depth treatment of the issues in the second stage of the Synod to take place the following year. It is interesting that, in contrast to the preparatory *instrumentum laboris*, which addressed the questions of canonically irregular marriages and streamlining canonical process in a fairly concise manner (§§92–102), the Synod Report devoted considerably more space to the Church's teaching and practice in this fundamental area.

On October 14th, at the outset of the gathering, Pope Francis emphasized the need to return regularly to the source of Church teaching, Jesus Christ, when addressing contemporary challenges in the area of marriage.

> The decisive condition is to maintain a fixed gaze on Jesus Christ, to pause in contemplation and in adoration of his Face....Indeed, every time we return to the source of the Christian experience, new paths and undreamed of possibilities open up.[8]

In this initial context, the Synod wasted no time in getting down to the crux of the question: "We need to understand the *newness* of the Sacrament of Marriage *in continuity with* natural marriage in its origin, that is, the manner of God's saving action in both creation and the Christian life" (emphasis added).[9]

SACRAMENTAL MARRIAGE AND THE RESTORATION OF NATURAL MARRIAGE

While the Report's initial observation about the "newness" of the sacrament carefully selects the phrase "*in continuity with* natural marriage," the next paragraph (14) "identifies" the sacramental marriage of baptized persons with natural marriage as restored by Jesus:

Jesus himself, referring to the original plan of the human couple, reaffirms the indissoluble union between a man and a woman and says to the Pharisees that "for your hardness of heart Moses allowed you to divorce your wives, but from the beginning it was not so" (*Mt* 19:8).

Relying on the words in Matthew's Gospel, the Synod asserts that "the fullness of revelation" by Christ "restores the original divine plan" regarding marriage. Such analysis raises a fundamental question: Is the revelation of Christ about marriage simply a "*return*" to what was, or is it somehow "*new*"?

The Synod develops its idea of "restoration" by distinguishing "three basic stages in God's plan for marriage and the family" (15–16):

1. The original, pre-sin, family represented by Adam and Eve in the Garden of Eden (Gen 1:27–28; 2:24);
2. The "historical" form of marriage in which the Mosaic bill of divorce was permitted for hardness of heart (Deut 24:1ff.);
3. The "restored marriage" proclaimed by Christ, in which the "spousal covenant, originating in creation and revealed in the history of salvation, receives its full meaning in Christ and his Church."

This crucial analysis of marriage's sacramentality and indissolubility, however, begs the question of the sacrament's "newness." To put it in older terminology: Is there any difference between the "preternatural" state of marriage in the Garden of Eden and the "supernatural" state of marriage among the baptized? Is it simply a "restoration" of what was, or does the new covenant of grace bestow on humanity the gift of marriage as a sacrament with a deeper meaning? To use the synodal words: Is marriage's "full meaning" a return to stage one, or does "full" mean "more"? It is not clear.

The documentary basis for the Synod's reflection on marriage as a sacramental vocation solidly rests on *Gaudium et Spes* (47–52), particularly its description of marriage as a community of life and love. Consequently, the Synod strongly emphasizes the need for faith in those who are encountering Christ in the sacrament of matrimony. "Christ the Lord 'comes into the lives of married Christians through the Sacrament of Matrimony,' and remains with them" (17, citing GS 48). "By living out the love that Christ has purified and brought to fulfillment, spouses are "consecrated and, through his grace, they build up the Body of Christ and are a domestic church" (17, citing LG 11).

The Synod also relies on the refinement of the doctrine on marriage and the family in postconciliar papal teaching: Paul VI in *Humanae Vitae*; John Paul II in *Gravissimum Sane* and *Familiaris Consortio*; Benedict XVI in *Deus Caritas Est*, 11: sacramental marriage as "the icon of the relationship between God and his people and vice versa. God's way of loving becomes the measure of human love"; Francis in *Lumen Fidei*, 53: "Encountering Christ...will not disappoint. Faith...makes us aware of a magnificent calling, the vocation of love."

The Synod does draw some distinction between sacramental marriage and natural marriage in a section titled "The Indissolubility of Marriage and the Joy of Sharing Life Together," grounding sacramental self-giving in the grace of baptism. The couple's vows promise "a total self-giving, faithfulness and openness to new life. The married couple recognizes these elements as constitutive in marriage, gifts offered to them by God, which they take seriously in their mutual commitment, in God's name and in the presence of the Church" (21).

The reference to baptism raises the question of the relationship of faith and marital consent: "Faith facilitates the possibility of assuming the benefits of marriage as commitments which are sustainable through the help of the grace of the Sacrament" (21). In the end, indissolubility results from the consecration by God of the couple's mutual love. God "confirms the indissoluble character of their love, offering them assistance to live their faithfulness, mutual complementarity and openness to new life" (21). Later in the Report, the Synod tentatively notes that "the role which faith plays in persons who marry could possibly be examined in ascertaining the validity of the Sacrament of Marriage, all the while maintaining that the marriage of two baptized Christians is always a sacrament" (48).

Natural marriage is neither defined nor described insofar as the primary focus of the Synod is on sacramental marriage. It is, however, affirmed as valid and sacred. "Valid elements...exist in some forms outside of Christian marriage—based on a stable and true relationship of a man and a woman—which, in any case, might be oriented towards Christian marriage" (22). In another section, however, the Synod echoes the traditional distinction between the marriages of two baptized persons of faith and other marriages when it states, "The only marriage bond for those who are baptized is sacramental and any breach of it is against the will of God." Emphasizing the special calling of the baptized, however, the Synod quickly adds, "At the same time, the Church is conscious of the weakness of many of her children who are struggling in their journey of faith" (24).

CANONICAL PROCESS AND THE RECEPTION OF COMMUNION

Turning to process, the Synod recognizes the need to streamline canonical procedures for those who are in irregular marriages because of the existence of a previous, presumably valid bond. Various suggestions were offered for consideration to make the process "more accessible and less time-consuming": dispensing the need for first-instance sentences to be confirmed in second instance, allowing cases to be handled administratively under the authority of the diocesan bishop, and setting up a simplified process for obvious cases of nullity (48). These suggestions, however, met with considerable resistance from some of the Synod fathers. Although the proposal was passed with significant support, the Report's addendum reveals that more negative votes were cast in this matter than in the voting on most other paragraphs: 143 in favor; 35 against.

When the Synod moved in paragraph 52 from process to the reception of communion, an even greater resistance emerged.

> Some synod fathers insisted on maintaining the present regulations, because of the constitutive relationship between participation in the Eucharist and communion with the Church as well as the teaching on the indissoluble character of marriage. Others expressed a more individualized approach, permitting access in certain situations and with certain well-defined conditions, primarily in irreversible situations and those involving moral obligations towards children who would have to endure unjust suffering.

The Synod went on to suggest,

> Access to the sacraments might take place if preceded by a penitential practice, determined by the diocesan bishop. The subject needs to be thoroughly examined, bearing in mind the distinction between an objective sinful situation and extenuating circumstances, given that "imputability and responsibility for an action can be diminished or even nullified by ignorance, inadvertence, duress, fear, habit, inordinate

attachments, and other psychological or social factors" (*Catechism of the Catholic Church* 1735).

The Report's addendum shows that paragraph 52 proved to be the most controversial of all, passing with the narrowest margin in the Report: only 104 votes in favor, 74 votes against.

In the end, the Synod emphasized that its Report is in no way a "final word."

> These proposed reflections...are intended to raise questions and indicate points of view which will later be developed and clarified through reflection in the local Churches in the intervening year leading to the XIV Ordinary General Assembly of the Synod of Bishops, scheduled for October, 2015, to treat *The Vocation and Mission of the Family in the Church and in the Contemporary World.* These are not decisions taken nor are they easy subjects. (52)

C. DIVORCE AND REMARRIAGE

The Church's concern about divorce and remarriage is not new. The early Church, the Middle Ages, the Council of Trent—all weighed in. It was not, however, until the modern world and secularism emerged over the last two centuries that the problem became more pressing.

HISTORICAL CONSIDERATIONS

The first general divorce law in England was not enacted until 1857. Even then, it was not until the twentieth century that the divorce rate grew geometrically. The Church began to offer some response to this crisis in the canonical field: the widening of the grounds of invalidity, particularly the lack of due discretion and the incapacity to assume the essential duties of marriage, a development forged by the Roman Rota and taken up in earnest by diocesan tribunals throughout the world, particularly after the teaching of Vatican Council II. These grounds were codified in canon 1095, 2°–3°, of the Code of Canon Law of 1983:

> The following are incapable of contracting marriage: 1° those who lack the sufficient use of reason; 2° those who suffer from a grave defect of discretion of judgment concerning the essential matrimonial rights and duties mutually to be handed over and accepted; 3° those who are not able to assume the essential obligations of marriage for causes of a psychic nature.

It is clear today that the emergence of widespread divorce and sequential marriages represents a paradigm shift in human behavior. As mentioned above, solutions proposed prior to and during the Synod still rely on the former paradigm. Some react to the crisis as an attack on a sacrosanct position that must be defended rather than an opportunity to revisit the paradigm. Others argue for a change in pastoral practice without really altering the underlying principles. Both sides recite, like a mantra, the conclusion that no sacramental marriage, once consummated, can be dissolved by any power on earth. Still, one must recall the preparatory admonition of Cardinal Lorenzo Baldisseri, the Secretary General of the Synod:

> "The Church is not timeless, she lives amidst the vicissitudes of history and the Gospel must be known and experienced by people today." Updating the Church's doctrine should pertain to the Church's teaching on divorce, the situation of divorcees and people who are in civil partnerships.[10]

Does this crisis not represent an *unprecedented* wake-up call: an opportunity to subject the paradigm itself to intense scrutiny? It does. But if one expects to update the paradigm, a crucial element will be to disentangle the essential theological meaning of marriage entrusted as a divine gift to the Church (sacramental marriage *in se*) from the theological interpretations and the ecclesiastical (and civil) laws that surround, enforce, protect, and foster that meaning in practice. This is easier said than done: there is no bright line between the sacramental reality and the canonical propositions, theological and juridical, that express it in a logical framework.

The very purpose of canon law, in its original articulation and its periodic renewal, is to be faithful to the sacramental reality by guiding practice and behavior in a way that will facilitate the grace of the sacrament in redeeming individuals, the Church, and the world. This is quite a challenge in any age, for while revelation and the sacraments of salvation are infinite mystery, our poor canonical attempts at implementation of that reality are frustratingly finite. That is, in fact, the lifeblood of an incarnational Church, expressing the Divine in human terms, taking what Christ won for us on the cross and gave to us freely, and rediscovering it in our own way in our own time, while remaining faithful to it.

THE CHURCH'S "CANONICAL CONSTRUCT"

If we collect the central theological and juridical propositions about marriage into a unified whole, we might refer to this summary as a "canonical construct of marriage." It is a "construct" not because the Church has invented it from the whole cloth, but in the sense that it concretizes and delimits the elements of the sacramental gift of marriage that are relevant to pastoral practice. While this finite set of propositions does not completely comprehend the sacrament of marriage, it does guide the Church in making decisions about how

Christians marry, what rights and duties ensue from their commitment, and how the Church should address failed marriages and the parties' desire to marry again. There is, unfortunately, a temptation to treat every aspect of such a construct as divinely revealed and equal in weightiness. This temptation must be resisted. Much of the construct is a response to cultural needs—that is, taking what is divinely revealed and applying it in a practical way to current pastoral issues—yet, as Cardinal Baldisseri emphasized, times and such cultural needs change.

Canonical constructs are not new. The Church has been engaged in this necessary task for two millennia—in every aspect of Christian life. The problem is that, in the arena of marriage, this particular construct has not been dusted off for about eight hundred years. Except for minor housekeeping, it has not been reformed in a way that allows the sacrament of marriage to be, in this postmodern world of ours, what Christ intended it to be in every generation. As Pope Francis stressed in his opening discourse at the Synod, renewal requires a regular return to the source, Jesus Christ, so that one rediscovers in changing times the radical *newness* that the Son of God brought to all of us, including married couples, by becoming indissolubly "one flesh" with humanity as the Son of Mary.

Fifty years ago, Edward Schillebeeckx, in his seminal work *Marriage: Human Reality and Saving Mystery*, published during the Vatican Council, lamented the lack of theological reflection and doctrinal pronouncements concerning the sacrament of marriage once the ferment of the twelfth century subsided.

> The theologians of the later period of scholasticism...did not always fully appreciate the medieval background which had occasioned this juridical formalisation, with the result that the 'treatise on marriage' became a study of the juridically formalised constitution of marriage rather than a dogmatic study

of the whole reality of marriage. In this way, the theology of marriage developed into a theology of a juridical abstraction which was legitimate in itself, but which led to the neglect of the study of marriage as an anthropological datum—as what Aquinas called the *officium civilitatis*. The theology of marriage was thus able to help the canonists, but it was of scarcely any help in pastoral matters.[11]

Ironically, Schillebeeckx himself, who had intended to complement his treatment of marriage in Scripture and history with a systematic analysis, never did so. Theologizing about the sacramental meaning of marriage has been, at best, "sparse"—a conclusion shared by Karl Rahner, who noted that little attention has been paid to the crucial sacramental dimension.[12] In the last half century, at least at this most fundamental level, things have not improved.

The following seven statements are an arguable attempt to articulate the "canonical construct" in which we are interested: the central theological and juridical propositions underlying pastoral practice concerning marriage, divorce, and remarriage, all of which are articulated in some fashion in canon law:

1. A man and woman bring a marriage into existence when, with due discretion and freedom, they validly exchange consent (c. 1057).
2. The marriage of two validly baptized persons is by that very fact a sacrament (c. 1055 §2).
3. Once parties marry validly, they themselves do not have the power to dissolve their marriage (intrinsic indissolubility, c. 1056), nor does anyone else have the power to dissolve a marriage other than the Roman Pontiff in his exercise of vicarious power in certain cases (extrinsic indissolubility, c. 1056). Civil divorces do not dissolve the marriage bond;

they simply adjudicate civil effects such as maintenance, support, and child custody (c. 1059).

4. Following the decision of St. Paul in 1 Corinthians 7:12–16, a marriage in which neither party is validly baptized may be dissolved through the Pauline privilege when the proper conditions, including conversion and baptism of one of them, are present (cc. 1143–47).

5. A marriage in which at least one of the parties is not validly baptized can be dissolved by the Roman Pontiff in favor of the faith (CDF Norms, April 30, 2001; cc. 1148–50).

6. Even a sacramental marriage of two baptized persons can be dissolved by the Roman Pontiff if it is not yet physically consummated in a human fashion (c. 1142).

7. A sacramental marriage of two baptized persons, once it is properly consummated, cannot be dissolved for any reason whatsoever, even by the exercise of the pope's power as vicar of Christ (c. 1141). A person bound by such a marriage cannot validly marry another during the lifetime of his or her spouse (c. 1085 §1).

Except for some logical development concerning the Church's power over nonsacramental or nonconsummated unions, this construct is essentially the same as that finalized in the Middle Ages. It served the Church well for many years, particularly concerning sacramentality and indissolubility. The problem, as with any canonical construct, is that theological and juridical formulations can be limited in scope and historically conditioned: specifically in the case of marriage, much of the construct on which pastoral practice has been based was forged mainly in the crucible of the twelfth-century consent-copula controversy, eventually settled in compromise fashion by Pope Alexander III (discussed in greater detail below).

Framed by the juridical questions of that age, the propositions incorporated a certain imbalance, a rather crucial lack of equilibrium. This imbalance is not about indissolubility itself. It is about the interrelationship of various kinds of marriage, about stages within the formation of marriage, and *a fortiori* about indissoluble marriage. It is precisely here that intense scrutiny is required, distinguishing the essence of Christ's teaching about marriage from historically conditioned interpretations and applications.

As Robert Imbelli, emeritus professor of theology at Boston College, wrote recently in *America*,

> The "divine pedagogy," which the synod report extols, builds upon the primordial relation of man and woman and leads it to its consummation in Christian marriage, wherein it sacramentalizes the spousal covenant between Christ and his beloved, the church.
>
> Such is the radical newness of Christian marriage that the church's doctrinal tradition celebrates and serves. Hence, it would be a grave error to dissociate "doctrine" and "pastoral practice." The latter must be rooted in the former and find its meaning and justification there. Of course, Christian doctrine is not reducible to propositions, since doctrine only seeks to illumine the mystery of Christ. Doctrines are, of their very nature, "mystagogic": leading into the mystery of Christ "in whom are hidden all the treasures of wisdom and knowledge" (Col 2:3).[13]

While conflicting pastoral approaches prior to and in the Synod's deliberations marshal reasonable arguments and cite authoritative voices from the Scriptures and Church teaching, they remain fundamentally conclusory, failing to address forthrightly the deeper questions underlying their positions, something that must be done if there is ever to be a solution that respects both divine revelation and authentic pastoral care. In today's world, the central issues that need airing are (1) extrinsic indissolubility, (2) the notion of consummation, and (3) the way that canonical process can be significantly altered.

D. INDISSOLUBILITY AND SACRAMENTALITY

THE NEW TESTAMENT

Indissolubility is deeply rooted in the revelation of Christ, inextricably intertwined with that great μυστήριον of the incarnation (Eph 5:32). The New Testament shows that Jesus proclaimed a newness about the permanence of marriage that is startling: it certainly shook his disciples. Opposing both rabbinic interpretations of the time (the more lenient *Hillel* and the stricter *Shammai* schools), he did not mince words: "Whoever divorces his wife and marries another commits adultery against her," (Mark 10:11–12) and "he who marries a woman divorced from her husband commits adultery" (Luke 16:18). This rejection of the orderly bill of divorce found in Deuteronomic law (the *erwat dābār*), by which a husband could repudiate his wife, was profound (Deut 24:1–4).

"Christ—and, following his teaching, the early apostolic church—allowed no scope whatever for divorce. This was in complete contrast to the teaching of the Old Testament and in express opposition to the Law of Moses....It also ran directly against the practice of the whole ancient world."[14] In the Roman Empire at the time of Jesus, both spouses had the right to repudiate unilaterally or simply to agree to divorce by mutual consent, causing the phenomenon of divorce to reach "epidemic proportions."[15]

The oral tradition that gave rise to the New Testament accounts of Jesus' teaching is extraordinarily solid. The pericopes on marriage in the three Synoptic accounts and the references in Paul's writings are close in consistency and as conclusive as one could expect. The scripture scholar John Meier, after an exhaustive treatment of the issue, puts it this way:

> The criteria of multiple attestation of sources and forms, of discontinuity and embarrassment, and of coherence all argue in favor of the historical Jesus issuing a prohibition of divorce as part of his halakic teaching. No criterion argues against historicity. Indeed, Jesus' prohibition of divorce is perhaps the single best-attested teaching in what we call his *hălăkâ*.[16]

Meier's analysis corroborates the conclusions of Raymond Collins:

> Anyone who reads the New Testament with an open mind must surely admit that the tradition of Jesus' having uttered a statement on divorce is well attested. It appears in four different books of the New Testament, in five different versions, and in a variety of literary forms, specifically a conflict story, an isolated saying, and a letter. No matter what one's approach to the criterion of multiple attestation, one must acknowledge that the tradition satisfies the requirements of this criterion for an authentic saying of Jesus....The diversity of expression given to this saying by the various New Testament authors shows that it was not a saying created by the early church in order to satisfy its internal needs. Rather it is clear that a traditional saying has been variously adapted by these different writers in order to make the tradition conformable to the real-life situation of the communities for which they were writing....The tradition of Jesus' teaching on divorce seems to enjoy as much claim to authenticity as

does any other part of his teaching. Indeed, E. P. Sanders has called it "the most securely attested saying by Jesus."[17]

Any solution to today's crisis cannot succeed if it does not incorporate an authentic understanding of the "newness" of Christian marriage, instituted by Christ himself. Absolute indissolubility, both intrinsic and extrinsic, is clearly part of this newness.

TRENT

Fourteen centuries later, the Council of Trent was very careful, when speaking about indissolubility, to phrase its canon 7 in a way that would show sensitivity to the practice of Eastern Christians: "If someone should say that the Church errs when it has taught and teaches, in accordance with scriptural and apostolic doctrine...."[18] Nonetheless, if one critically reexamines the tradition from the Scriptures—Jewish, Greek, and Latin—through the fathers and medievalists, right up to modern and postmodern times, could one really argue convincingly for the abandonment of the intrinsic and extrinsic indissolubility of Christian marriage? One could not—and one should not, *provided* that indissolubility is properly understood and applied in the concrete.

For indissolubility is not the *only* hallmark of the newness of Christian marriage. The *sacramentality* of the indissoluble marriage of the baptized is essential to the Church's life. It is not some peripheral aspect of ecclesial life; it is intimately connected with the very presence of the God-man among us, never to leave us, indissolubly joined to us, the central Christ event, inserted into the fabric of society and the Church, the family.

The "one flesh" that the spouses become (the important term of both the Jewish and Christian Scriptures) symbolizes the incarnational union of the Son of God with humanity and, like all the sacraments, brings about that which it symbolizes. Although marriage as a symbol of Christ and the Church traces its roots back to the Scriptures, the idea that this is a form of "sacramentality" in the strict sense arose rather late in the Church's history.

Almost all the elements of the canonical construct of marriage, including absolute indissolubility, were in place by the twelfth century—but not strict sacramentality. Symbolism? Yes. Sacramentality? No. Even though, as we look at the entire canonical construct, sacramentality logically underlies and explains indissolubility, it was not put forward as an essential element of indissolubility until afterward. This may be one of the reasons that sacramentality, although the bedrock of the "newness" of marriage in Christ, has received relatively little theological and canonical development.

Trent listed marriage among the seven true and proper sacraments of the new law instituted by Christ, but it did not offer much of an explanation about its sacramental nature.[19] Nonetheless, the Council did affirm the substantial *newness* that Christ gave to all seven sacraments, distinguishing them *essentially* from the "sacraments" of the old Law as more than simply revised ceremonies and external rites.[20] Unfortunately, our canonical construct has failed to plumb the depths of the sacramentality of marriage and, over time, has ended up giving it rather short shrift.

REDUCTIONISM TO NATURAL MARRIAGE

Consider, for example, the austere character of the second proposition of our canonical construct, in which sacramentality is, for all practical purposes, reduced to the fact of two valid baptisms: *When both parties are validly baptized, their marriage is by that very fact a sacrament.* This assertion can be found in canon 1055 §2, which repeats word-for-word a statement in the prior Code of Canon Law, promulgated in 1917 (CIC 17, c. 1012 §2): "*A valid matrimonial contract cannot exist between the baptized without it being by that fact a sacrament.*" The inclusion of this older formula in canon 1055 is an unfortunate example of the Code's tendency to avoid theological debate: it forces into the old wineskin of paragraph 2 the new wine of paragraph 1's deeply theological description of marriage as covenant, drawn verbatim from Vatican II's *Gaudium et Spes*, 48:

> The matrimonial covenant by which a man and a woman establish between themselves a partnership of the whole of life and which is ordered by its nature to the good of the spouses and the procreation and education of offspring, has been raised by Christ the Lord to the dignity of a sacrament between the baptized (c. 1055 §1).

This reduction to two valid baptisms not only avoids the question of the relation of faith and sacrament but even forces conclusions about the validity of marriage that are strained, to say the least. The radical identification of sacrament with the contract of the baptized leads to the conclusion that words like *sacrament* or *communion* are juridically superfluous: they have no more impact on the juridical elements of validity than to point out that the parties who are positing marital consent are validly baptized. Insofar as consent alone makes marriage, equation of contract and sacrament means that the marital consent of the baptized *does not differ* from the marital consent of those who are not baptized: the object of marital consent, that to which the parties are consenting, is essentially the same for every marriage, sacramental or natural, a conclusion that appears in a number of Rotal decisions.[21]

THE 1983 REVISION OF THE CODE

The tug-of-war between contract and sacrament pops up in other areas as well. The following are a few examples from the debate that went on within the Pontifical Commission for the Revision of the Code of Canon Law of this reductionist thinking:

1. When the committee on marriage discussed the idea of including as a ground of nullity of marriage the "incapacity to assume the essential obligations of marriage" (which eventually became c. 1095 §3), a certain wording was justified because it simply represented a *codification of the natural law*. In other words, there is no difference between natural marriage and sacramental marriage in the area of marriage's essential obligations.[22]

2. The same idea made the Code Commission hesitant to include as an essential obligation of marriage even the conciliar phrase "communion of life," considering such a phrase so closely linked to sacramentality that it might be misinterpreted as broadening the "essence" of marriage. Thus the phrase "the right to those things that essentially constitute the communion of life" proposed for what would eventually be canon 1101 was replaced with the generic phrase "some essential element of marriage."[23]

3. The promulgated version of canon 1101 §2 actually deleted the phrase "sacramental dignity" when speaking of invalidating exclusions of the will (even though it had been approved by the Code Commission at its *plenarium* of October 1981) on the basis that it was superfluous insofar as a spouse's exclusion of "sacramental dignity" is

nothing other than "total simulation" since every marriage of two baptized persons is, as stated in canon 1055 §2, *by that very fact* a sacrament.[24]

These examples may seem very technical, but the stance that they represent is foundational: it results in certain canonical conclusions that affect the pastoral life of individuals, including the ironic assertion that the sacramentality of marriage is operative *even if the parties do not know that they were baptized.* Can two people whose "faith" is limited to the theological virtue infused by valid baptism and who have no awareness, much less practice, of that faith participate in the "celebration" of a Christian marriage—that is, minister the sacrament by giving and receiving each other (c. 1057 §2)? And what about those who, though aware of their baptism, consciously and purposely *reject* faith, perhaps even profess atheism? Do they enter a sacramental marriage when they exchange marital consent with another baptized person? Or to put it negatively, if the contracting parties are clearly opposed to the very idea that a marriage is sacramental, are they, in fact, *unable to marry validly* because they are not properly disposed to posit the consent that is necessary for a sacramental *matrimonium in fieri*?

DEROGATION OF THE FORMAL ACT EXEMPTIONS

This dilemma was one of the inconsistencies in pastoral practice that resulted from the ill-fated inclusion in the Code of the "formal act" exemptions and led eventually to their deletion. In the original wording of the 1983 Code, if a Catholic formally abandoned the faith, he or she would be exempted from the law prohibiting mixed marriage and from the requirement to be married by a priest or deacon. Thus, if such a person married a baptized non-Catholic in a civil ceremony, or even another Catholic who had formally abandoned the faith, the two of them would still be viewed as "celebrating" the *sacrament* of matrimony.

Or would they? The formal decision to depart the Church might very well indicate the formal rejection of all sacraments. Insofar as the corollary of canon 1055 §2 seems to be "if the marriage is valid, it is a sacrament; but if the marriage fails to be a sacrament, it is invalid," their consent would end up being invalid in any case. The derogations in 2009 of the marriage exemptions arising from a formal act of abandonment may simply have been a response to the impracticality that emerged since their introduction into the 1983 Code.[25] Yet, one might see in such derogations a distancing in canon law from the conciliar concept of religious liberty and from any juridic role for personal faith in regard to marital sacramentality.

This kind of reasoning raises a nagging question: Have the right to marry and the Vatican Council's teaching on religious liberty been abolished in these cases? Has the Church's canonical construct caused her to take the position that two baptized persons who, maliciously or even innocently, decline to celebrate marriage as a sacrament will either have their wishes ignored, settling them, perhaps unwittingly or unwillingly, in a sacramental marriage, or be prevented from marrying validly since they lack the minimum right intention? Many, including the International Theological Commission, the 1980 Synod of Bishops, John Paul II, Benedict XVI, and the prelate auditors of the Roman Rota, have struggled with this quandary.

THE 1978 MEETING OF THE INTERNATIONAL THEOLOGICAL COMMISSION

In 1978, the International Theological Commission (ITC) issued *Propositions on the Doctrine of Christian Marriage*, articulating the horns of the dilemma: sacramentality and indissolubility are in a "reciprocal, constitutive relationship" (2.2).[26] The ITC was hesitant to contradict the canonical identification of the marriage contract of baptized persons with the sacrament (3.3).

The ITC was therefore forced to conclude that nonbelieving baptized persons enter a relationship that, "even if it resembles marriage, cannot in any way be recognized by the church as a non-sacramental conjugal society. For the church, no natural marriage separated from the sacrament exists for baptized persons, but only natural marriage elevated to the dignity of a sacrament" (3.5). Yet, the ITC left room for doctrinal and juridical development by asserting that the Church "can further define the concepts of sacramentality and consummation, by explaining them even better, so that the whole doctrine on the indissolubility of marriage can be put forward in a deeper and more precise presentation" (4.4).

THE 1980 SYNOD OF BISHOPS ON THE CHRISTIAN FAMILY

The ITC propositions clearly influenced the deliberations of the 1980 Synod of Bishops on the Christian Family, which also raised the same question without resolving it. Among the forty-three resolutions and proposals transmitted to Pope John Paul II on October 24, 1980, was Proposition 12d:

> We must further investigate whether the statement that a valid marriage between baptized persons is always a sacrament is also applicable for those who have lost the faith. This will then entail juridical and pastoral consequences. Above all it must be investigated what the pastoral criteria might be for discerning the faith of the engaged couple and how much their intention

of doing what the Church does more or less should include the minimal intention of believing with the Church as well.[27]

JOHN PAUL II

In 1981, John Paul II encountered this dilemma in the apostolic exhortation that followed the Synod, *Familiaris Consortio*: "When in spite of all efforts engaged couples show that they reject explicitly and formally what the Church intends to do when the marriage of baptized persons is celebrated, the pastor of souls cannot admit them to the celebration of marriage" (68). The implication is that, if they were admitted, their consent would be invalid, although *Familiaris Consortio* refrained from stating that explicitly. This reticence avoided an ecumenical problem, for to say so explicitly would suggest to validly baptized non-Catholics (many of whom do not in any way whatsoever accept the sacramentality of marriage) that, if their faith were deficient, they would lack the minimum intention to marry validly their non-Catholic baptized spouse in their own Christian ceremony.

Pope John Paul II retained an intense interest in this topic. Twenty years later, in his address to the Rota (February 1, 2001), he touched on subjective faith and marital consent, noting that, while the Church proposes "a *new* estimation of [marriage's] natural dimension," it is proposing *nothing more* than what existed "according to God's plan from the 'beginning'" (emphasis added).[28]

This is another formulation of the dilemma: How are we to assert the "newness" that Christ brought to Christian marriage without denying its identity with natural marriage? Is marriage "old" or is it "new"? Is it "really new" or is it "nothing more" than ever before? Is the newness only in the effects of the sacrament but not in the sign itself and its creation through marital consent? The 2014 Synod's attempt once again to address the mystery of sacramental marriage by distinguishing three stages in God's plan for marriage and the family, as was mentioned above, falls prey to the same tension (15–16).

BENEDICT XVI

Pope Benedict XVI addressed the same quandary in his address to the Roman Rota on January 26, 2013:

> The indissoluble pact between a man and a woman does not, for the purposes of the sacrament, require of those engaged to be married, their personal faith; what it does require, as a necessary minimal condition, is the intention to do what the Church does. However, if it is important not to confuse the problem of the intention with that of the personal faith of those contracting marriage, it is nonetheless impossible to separate them completely.

Near the end of his address, however, he notes that one "must not, therefore, disregard the consideration that can arise in the cases in which, precisely because of the absence of faith, the good of the spouses is jeopardized, that is, excluded from the consent itself...." His conclusion is another indication of how restrictive the Church's canonical construct is, even for the pope:

> With these reflections, I certainly do not intend to suggest any facile automatism between the lack of faith and the invalidity of the matrimonial union, but rather to highlight how such a lack may, although not necessarily, also damage the goods of the marriage, since the reference to the natural order desired by God is inherent in the conjugal pact (cf. Gen 2:24).[29]

THE ROMAN ROTA

Rotal judges and diocesan tribunals have struggled with the same question when dissecting the elements for the validity of marital consent. "Sacramental dignity" is a *special property* of the marriage of the baptized; but, in the end, the Church's canonical construct requires that it be viewed, unlike other marital properties, as *indistinguishable from the marriage itself*. Not that Rotal judges do not try to make the distinction!

Rotal auditor Msgr. Jose M. Serrano Ruiz has sought to categorize as a separate ground the exclusion of the sacramental dignity of marriage, a ground that is applicable only if both parties are baptized. Rather than identify exclusion of sacramental dignity with total exclusion of the marriage itself, he has tried in some cases to isolate the positive act of the will against sacramentality to the extent that the nullity is seen to arise not from some sort of total simulation (in sacramental clothing) but from the specific lack of faith and, even more convincingly, from the party's animosity to faith and to any notion of the divine. Serrano Ruiz bases his rationale on the teaching of *Gaudium et Spes*, the propositions of the International Theological Commission, and the implications of religious liberty in *Dignitatis Humanae*.[30]

Other Rotal auditors, however, reject Serrano Ruiz's approach. Rotal auditor Msgr. Kenneth Boccafola, relying on the work of Cardinal Mario Pompedda, termed the matrimonial contract and the matrimonial sacrament "forms (*modi*)—the one natural, the other supernatural—of the very same reality." The sacramental dignity of a marriage is "nothing other than the natural bond itself between baptized spouses....It is the 'res' of matrimony that becomes 'res et sacramentum' among the baptized....Sacramentality then adds nothing to the natural covenant."[31]

What about marriages of those whose value system is "anti-sacramentality/anti-indissolubility"? Do they directly and principally intend error when they marry or possibly exclude the permanence every party must intend? When dealing with error or an invalidating intention, can one actually distinguish an "absolute" act of the will and a "hypothetical" act of the will? Rotal auditor Giuseppe Sciacca tried to do so:

> An exclusion…can be either absolute, when the contractant excludes the indissoluble bond entirely and in every way whatsoever, or hypothetical, when, e.g., the contractant, because of excessive anxiety about the eventual outcome of his marriage, rejects the perpetuity of the marriage at the very moment of forming consent if the situation should occur, namely, if things turn out badly, always keeping for himself an open door: in this regard, however, it is very important to note that the exclusion, which is clearly present at the origin of the consent and renders it invalid, is not hypothetical; the only thing that is hypothetical is the concrete event of the breakup of the invalidly-entered pseudo-marriage.[32]

It seems to be a distinction without a difference. And yet, does it not seem appropriate to differentiate in a real way the marital consent of those entering a sacramental union from others? One of the predominant psychological grounds of nullity is incapacity to consent because of the lack of due discretion (c. 1095, 2°). Considering the essential link of sacramentality and indissolubility, is it so unreasonable to conclude that those who enter an absolutely indissoluble (i.e., sacramental and consummated) marriage must have *greater deliberative capacity* and a *higher degree of freedom* to will such an irreversible chain of events than one would require of a couple who are entering a nonsacramental marriage that can, under certain circumstances, be dissolved? Judges hesitate to assert this distinction: the canonical construct within which they work will not allow it. They are constrained by the proposition that a sacramental marriage is simply a natural marriage that happens to be contracted by two validly baptized persons.

THE NEWNESS OF THE SACRAMENT OF MATRIMONY

All of this, however, begs the question. Contrary to the spare canonical construct, *everything* about a sacramental marriage, the marriage of the *new* covenant, is supposed to be "elevated," "greater," "radically new"—to use Pope John Paul II's words. In *Familiaris Consortio*, he quotes his own Address to the Delegates of the Centre de Liaison des Equipees de Recerche (November 3, 1979):

In a word, it is a question of the normal characteristics of all *natural* conjugal love, *but* with a *new significance* which not only purifies and strengthens them, but *raises* them to the extent of making them the expression of *specifically Christian* values. (13, emphasis added)

The pope goes on to highlight the *ongoing growth* that a sacramental marriage should entail:

The gift of the Spirit is a commandment of life for Christian spouses and at the same time a stimulating impulse so that every day they may progress towards an *ever richer* union with each other on all levels—of the body, of the character, of the heart, of the intelligence and will, of the soul—revealing in this way to the Church and to the world the *new* communion of love, given by the grace of Christ. (19, emphasis added)

Notice John Paul's struggle to identify "newness" and yet his hesitation to follow through on its ramifications. Why does that "new significance" introduced by Jesus not call for a "new" standard of judgment about *all* essential aspects of the matrimonial covenant—in other words, newness not merely in its effects (*matrimonium in facto esse*), but right at the start in the way that the sacramental marriage is created (*matrimonium in fieri*)? One obvious reason is that, to assert such "newness," one must modify the age-old canonical construct.

Like Pope John Paul II, the 2014 Synod has also been hesitant to do so. That is why the Synod Report falls back on the assertion that Jesus' words to the Pharisees in Matthew 19:8 are justification for identifying sacramental marriage with the original state of natural marriage. Such an interpretation does not distinguish intrinsic and extrinsic indissolubility nor does it give sufficient emphasis to the radical newness that the "fullness of revelation" brings to the entire new covenant, including the sacrament of marriage.[33]

These examples point to a lack of balance, an "in-equilibrium" that the postmodern crisis in marriage makes more and more obvious and neuralgic. Sacramentality and indissolubility are stifled in today's world by the austerity of the Church's canonical construct of marriage. The truth about marriage revealed by Christ is struggling to be set free, to be given some breathing room in today's concrete cultural scene, so that marriage will indeed be part of Christ's new covenant, signifying it and, at the same time, bringing it about, not in theory but in the real world of married couples who are baptized people of faith, hope, and love and who are called to form sacramentally with their children an interpersonal communion and ministry of life and love.

A juridical understanding of absolute indissolubility is not enough. Unless one is willing to separate it from sacramentality, to reduce it simply to an add-on, a kind of legal positivism, it will be increasingly difficult for the current *canonical construct* of theological interpretations and judicial propositions to do justice to the *mystery* of indissoluble Christian marriage. Viewing a marriage covenant that has been immersed in the incarnation, death, and resurrection of Christ as identical to a union that is not part of the sacramental life of the Church, except for certain strictly juridical effects, is simply going to be more and more untenable.

Ironically, however, the Church's revered canonical tradition itself may very well point to a way that the newness of Christian marriage, including its properties of sacramentality and indissolubility, can be viewed more dynamically.

E. CONSUMMATION

Thirty-six years ago, the International Theological Commission explicitly noted that further development must take place in regard to the assertion that the valid marriage of two validly baptized spouses does not become absolutely indissoluble unless and until they *consummate* it by engaging in an act of sexual intercourse.[34] To understand the crucial role that consummation plays in the Church's canonical construct of marriage and whether some modern development can be crafted, one must journey back seven centuries to the age in which this proposition was canonically formulated.

THE TWELFTH-CENTURY COMPROMISE

The idea that a marriage is consummated presents another lack of balance in the canonical construct of marriage, one whose explanation is much clearer insofar as its origins extend back to the twelfth century. This building block of the canonical construct dates back to Pope Alexander III's compromise resolution of the consent-copula controversy, epitomized by the differing positions of Gratian in Bologna and Peter Lombard in Paris. Alexander III retained elements from both theories and, in doing so, created a theoretical problem; a problem, however, which might very well turn out to be a farsighted opportunity for authentic development, leading to a fuller understanding of the meaning of Christian marriage.

Gratian held a mitigated copula theory: for him and his followers, marriage "begins" with consent or with multiple consents of varying types—some espousal, some marital—but it is not "completed" until the spouses seal their consent by an act of sexual intercourse (*copula carnalis*).[35]

Peter Lombard, on the other hand, gave little, if any, meaning to *copula carnalis*—perhaps an additional form of symbolism of the union of Christ and the Church, but *no juridic effects*, even as to indissolubility. For Lombard and his followers, an unconsummated marriage represents the union of Christ and the Church by will and by charity; physical consummation adds only the *representation* of Christ's incarnational union with the Church. Of juridical interest to the Paris school, instead, was the critical distinction among the various kinds of consent (a distinction to which Gratian gave much less juridic weight): *consensus per verba de futuro* (the promise to marry) in contrast to *consensus per verba de praesenti* (the act of consenting to marriage). Once the latter words are exchanged, with or without formalities and/or blessings (recall that this is the age of "clandestine marriages"), the marriage that is brought into being is absolutely indissoluble.[36]

Central to both theories was the protection of the validity of the *Gottesmutterehe*, the unconsummated marriage of Mary and Joseph: something that was much easier for Lombard to defend than for

Gratian.[37] Their different explanations, however, were not merely academic; they represented different pastoral practices north and south of the Alps.

Alexander III (1159–81) settled the divergent decision making of tribunals that were following one or the other of these theories, by opting fundamentally for the Parisian solution but pragmatically adding a compromise element from Bologna. "Alexander attributed to consummation a new position in the formation of the bond. It was neither all-important as Gratian claimed, nor inconsequential as Lombard taught, but enjoyed a perfective or complementary function which rendered the marriage indissoluble."[38] The compromise nature of this settlement, however, lacked a certain consistency and theoretical balance: "a certain lack of equilibrium that will be felt in all subsequent ages."[39]

In a way, this foundational discrepancy and lack of equilibrium reflects the age-old contest between the spiritual and the physical. A marital relationship is not purely spiritual: it involves sexuality in the fullest sense. Human beings are "fleshed souls," not bodiless spirits.[40] Even the consent that they exchange is not purely spiritual: it has no juridic effect, even in clandestine marriages, without being physically expressed by words or other signs (and, in the days prior to Trent, even by sexual intercourse itself when accompanied by *affectus maritalis*).

But the nagging question remains: If consent, from which all the theological and juridical effects of marriage flow, is manifested in words, why is an additional physical expression required? If a sacramental marriage is *fully* a marriage with the exchange of consent, how does a single act of physical intercourse render it "more indissoluble"? And if it is somehow "*more* indissoluble," is it also "*more* sacramental" (recall that Alexander III's resolution *preceded* the Church's affirmation of marriage's strict sacramentality)? It is clearly not "another" act of consent (even though canon 1061 §1 now states that it must be completed "in a human fashion"). Nor do modern theologians suggest that the consummated marriage participates *more fully* in the mystery of the union of Christ and his Church, as the medievalists taught about its symbolic function.

At the very least, one must explain how the Church can assert that the sacramental *marriage bond* is *formed by consent alone* and yet the sacramental bond's *absolute indissolubility* is *completed* by *consummation*, for her canonical construct asserts that the *ratum sed non consummatum* marriage is susceptible to *dissolution—despite the words of Christ* (the bedrock basis for both intrinsic and extrinsic indissolubility).

An interpretation that resolves somewhat the inconsistency of Alexander III's solution is to conclude that the Church has the right, in applying the teaching of Christ, to recognize *stages* in the formation of the fullness of sacramental marriage (the point at which the individual marriage fulfills the newness of Jesus' teaching). Both Peter Lombard and Gratian, although they differed on the endpoint, admitted that there were stages in the formation of the marriage bond, but for neither of them did the prior acts produce a "real" marriage; the prior acts were only preliminary.

Gratian used the words *perfectum* and *consummatum* interchangeably to differentiate the marriage whose formation had been "completed" by sexual intercourse (*matrimonium perfectum seu consummatum*) from the stage of the formation process in which marriage had only "begun" through the exchange of consent (*matrimonium initiatum*). But, for Gratian, the "begun" marriage was not a "real" marriage, just as the espousal by consent about the future was not a "real" marriage for Lombard. Though they differed on the moment when the "real" marriage came into being, both of them, from that moment on, considered it absolutely indissoluble.

AN EXPANDED NOTION OF "CONSUMMATION"

With Alexander III's compromise, however, one is required to conclude that there are stages *within* the formation of *indissoluble marriage itself*, rather than merely prior to it. Marriage, in fact sacramental marriage, is already present with consent; nothing more is needed. Yet, the marriage becomes qualitatively different when a second stage is reached, when the marriage is "completed" ("consummated") by a single act of physical intercourse. This kind of "completion" as explained by Alexander III differs significantly from the teaching of both Gratian and Lombard.

The question remains, however: Why must the Church continue to assert that a single act of marital intercourse is necessarily the juridical moment of completion? Despite the longevity of this canonical theory, it is time to abandon the reliance on the single physical act; it is a cultural element, introduced in the early Middle Ages, that no longer fulfills its function. For centuries, it was perfectly acceptable both juridically and symbolically, but it did not come to the Church's canonical construct from divine revelation. It finds no basis in Scripture unless one is willing to misinterpret the Genesis notion of *una caro* and the teaching of Paul in Ephesians to refer to physical intercourse rather than to the union of persons. Nor can it be ascribed to tradition, for to do so, is to ignore the legitimate development by the fathers and medievalists of marriage as indissoluble and sacramental (symbolic) apart from sexual acts.

The canonical historian James Brundage ascribes the heightened significance given to physical consummation as an attempt in the early Middle Ages "to harmonize the prevalent Germanic tradition with Christian teaching." Archbishop Hincmar of Reims (845–852), on whose writings Gratian heavily relied,

> made the most ambitious effort to do this. In a letter concerning a French marriage case about 860, Hincmar propounded a theory of marriage hitherto unknown in canon law, namely that an unconsummated marriage was incomplete and hence not fully binding…the writers whose words he appropriated and stitched together to suit his purposes would have been astonished at what he did with them, for Hincmar's coital theory of marriage was a novel attempt to give sexual consummation a central role in the formation of Christian marriage.[41]

Why would the first act of sexual intercourse have become so significant in the early Middle Ages? One must recall, first, that the Church had not yet mandated canonical form for the validity of marital consent. Clandestine marriages remained a problem for the Church and society. Though the Church often urged public consent and the priestly blessing, such form was not required for validity until the Council of Trent in the sixteenth century. Engaging in sexual intercourse was at least an objective act that seemed to settle any debate about whether a marriage had been created by the secret marital consent of the parties.

Further, the view of woman added to the mix. In many ways, the bride was still seen in many regards as a high form of "chattel," the object of a commercial transaction between her father and her husband. Once she and her husband had engaged in sexual intercourse, the deal was sealed; there was no possibility of rescinding it (a canonized form of *traditio rei* as the completion of a contract?). Although the Church stressed forcefully the need for consent by the woman, cultural forces resisted the idea that her voice was "equal" to the man's. The usual *weddung* was principally a pact between the bride's father or family and the husband, a form of "bride purchase." Once the exchange took place ritually and was sealed physically, a return of the woman to her father was impermissible.

Brundage gives a good sense of these attitudes by outlining the three legitimate methods of contracting marriage in early Germanic law:

> By capture (*Raubehe*), by purchase (*Kaufehe*) and by mutual consent (*Friedelehe*). Bride purchase involved an agreement between two families. An exchange of property was an essential part of *Kaufehe* and the Germanic law codes encouraged this type of marriage….It began with an agreement (*Muntvertrag*) between the suitor or his father and the father or guardian of the prospective bride, concerning the compensation to be paid to the woman's family by the groom's family…followed by a public transfer (*Anvertrauung*) of the bride to the head of the groom's family. This was followed by a wedding ritual (*Trauung*), during which the members of the bride's clan stood in a circle around her to witness the transfer and to signify their consent to the transaction. The process involved conveyance not only of the person of the bride to the family of the groom, but also of legal power (*Munt, mundium*) over her to the husband and his family group….This type of union, involving active participation and control by the families of the parties, was the preferred type of marriage.[42]

The cultural origin of the sexual act as the juridical completion of the indissoluble marriage bond may have been understandably appropriate for its time, but its incorporation by the Church into the formation of the sacramental marriage bond leads inexorably to the suggestion that, in today's highly different culture and *with a deeper personalist understanding of the object of marital consent*, the Church should be open to the notion that marriages pass through varied stages beyond sexual intercourse before *absolute indissolubility emerges*. In other words, using Gratian's terminology and Alexander III's compromise, the Church should still require that a process be "consummated" before the absolutely indissoluble sacramental marriage is "completed," but this "consummation" may not in every case be fulfilled simply by a single physical act. Successive stages of completion, yes; simply a physical act, no.

Such a modification makes sense when one reexamines the explicit shift in theology and canon law from the *ius in corpus* to the *persons themselves* as the *proper object of marital consent*.[43] Just as it was legitimate for centuries to consider the first exercise of the *ius in corpus* as the completion of the absolutely indissoluble bond, it seems eminently appropriate to require the *actuation of the interpersonal self-giving* to be accomplished before one can say that the spouses' mutual consent, which creates a valid sacramental marriage to begin with, is fully consummated, that is, *completed*, and therefore *absolutely* indissoluble? With some couples, this may occur immediately; with others it may be the fullness of self-giving that comes about over time; and some, while perhaps capable of the minimum discretion required for marital consent, unfortunately never achieve the unity required of a consummated sacramental marriage.

JUSTICIABILITY: JUDGING INVALIDITY AND/OR DISSOLUBILITY? DISSOLVING MARRIAGES THAT WERE NEVER COMPLETED

Some might object that such a proposition, by moving away from the physical act, offers no juridical moment or provable fact to warrant a judgment. At least, physical consummation or the lack of it has been, within reason, justiciable, determinable by legal process. Such an objection would make sense if applied to consent rather than consummation insofar as there must be a clear moment for the *initiation* of a valid sacramental marriage (one of the rationales for requiring canonical form). But when it comes to consummation, one is not speaking about *validity*—either of the marriage itself, or of the sacrament. One is speaking, rather, of the *completion* of the *indissolubility* (and, one might suggest, the *sacramentality*) of that marriage.

Any judgment about the accomplishment of that consummation or its failure to take place would have the advantage of the 20/20 vision provided by hindsight. While one might be hard pressed to describe *prospectively* what would go into the actualization of an interpersonal relationship for a particular couple, it may not be that difficult to determine that, when one *looks back* in light of the theological and canonical principles regarding the interpersonal nature of marriage, one must conclude that *it just never happened*.

After all, is this not the retrospective path to a couple's exchange of vows that judges currently travel to discover its deficiency? One of the great contributions of the Roman Rota and diocesan tribunals has been the development of research by psychological experts into the implications of the early life development and experiences of spouses prior to marriage as a basis, with postconsent behavior, to conclude that they lacked capacity or the proper intention to posit valid marital consent. The same skill set would prove invaluable in judging whether such spouses, even if they presumably posited valid marital consent (which itself might also be questionable), did or did not actually complete that sacramental formation required for an absolutely indissoluble union, that is, a union that fulfills the mandate set forth by Christ in the Scriptures for two Christians *giving themselves as persons of faith* to each other.

What if the tribunal's task were not merely to judge the validity of consent, but rather to examine whether the couple *ever* really became "one flesh" not only in the *physical* sense but in the *scriptural* sense (i.e., "one life"), both in their exchange of marital consent and in their completing of that consent by actualizing the oneness that *una caro* symbolizes? For the marriage of two baptized persons, the tribunal's quest would be sacramental rather than purely juridical: namely, whether the spouses ever rose to the level of mirroring the union of Christ and the Church in the incarnation to complete their indissoluble union.

This is a search in which the faith of the parties, or lack of it, would truly have a bearing. The search would not be limited to whether the lack of faith determined the will in regard to the properties of marriage or perhaps rendered the parties incapable of marital consent from the beginning. Instead, it would assess the level of faith of the parties as a very real element in the couple's *achievement of the completed marriage* that corresponds to Christ's teaching. Such an approach would expand the interplay of faith and marital commitment in response to the proposal of some of the Synod fathers: "The role which faith plays in persons who marry could possibly be examined in ascertaining the validity of the Sacrament of Marriage, all the while maintaining that the marriage of two baptized Christians is always a sacrament."[44]

In such a process, the marriage that was never brought to completion would, according to the Church's canonical tradition, be presumably valid but still susceptible to dissolution—by the current practice of papal dispensation. It would expand the discretion to resolve such marital situations that developed over the centuries. Prior to the exercise of papal power, the *ipso iure* dissolution of non-consummated marriages by the unilateral decision of one of the parties to enter religious life was already a very ancient tradition. Some date the use of papal power in such cases back to Martin V (1417–31) or even Alexander III (1159–81). John Noonan notes, "Finally, in 1741 Pope Benedict XIV (Prospero Lambertini), in *Dei miseratione*, exposed the marvelous power to the world at large. He kept the curial language which avoided shock: the Pope 'dispensed,' he did not 'dissolve.'" Noonan incisively concludes,

Seeking to centralize responsibility in the Pope, *Dei misera-tione* in effect confirmed the treatment of nonconsummation cases in the Curia. Incidentally, almost accidentally, nonetheless deliberately, it acknowledged at the highest level that a discretion existed and was employed to terminate one class of Christian marriage.[45]

It is clear from this history that the power over nonconsummated unions need not remain so centrally positioned. When the Code of Canon Law was being revised, the Commission considered decentralizing the process, modifying the relevant canon of the 1917 Code (c. 1119) to allow bishops to exercise such a faculty or at least to use the more generic phrase "by ecclesiastical authority" so as not to forestall theological discussion about the vicarious power of the pope and the possibility of its delegation. Others thought that the same power actually belongs to bishops by ordination. In the end, for practical reasons, the drafting committee decided that the exercise of this power should still be reserved in the revised Code to the Roman Pontiff (now c. 1142).[46]

Yet, there is a specific canon in the current Code which would serve as a basis for significant decentralization of such "dispensations." The Pauline privilege is applied on the diocesan level in the case of two separated unbaptized spouses, one of whom asks to be baptized and to marry another. Because of special difficulties in missionary lands, this form of dissolution, still handled on the local level, was extended to some other cases in favor of the faith. The 1917 Code incorporated these papal accommodations, particularly those issued in the sixteenth century (1917 Code c. 1125). Following this tradition, canon 1149 of the current Code explicitly permits a convert, after receiving baptism, to marry again even though it turns out that his or her spouse, separated irrevocably by captivity or persecution, *had in fact been baptized* after their separation. In such a case, it is not the pope, acting individually by vicarious power, but the new marriage that *ipso iure* dissolves the first marriage (as in the use of the standard Pauline privilege). This means that the marriage in question, at the moment of dissolution, is properly termed *ratum sed non consummatum*, a sacramental marriage (made sacramental by the baptisms of the two separated spouses) that has never been consummated. Clearly, if an expanded understanding of consummation is accepted, there are many ways that it can be implemented within the Church's tradition—the current practice of papal dispensation in favor of the faith; authorization of such decision making by diocesan bishops (as is done with the use of the Pauline privilege); even the delegation of such power to the judge in the individual case.

NOTES

1. Walter Kasper, "The Problem of the Divorced and Remarried," February 20, 2014, Eng. trans. Sandro Magister, www.chiesa.espressonline.it (March 1, 2014); also Walter Kasper, *The Gospel of the Family*, trans. William Madges (New York: Paulist Press, 2014).

2. Walter Kasper, "The Message of Mercy," *America* 211, no. 6 (September 15, 2014): 17.

3. Kasper, "The Problem of the Divorced."

4. *Proceedings of the Thirty-Seventh Annual Convention of the Canon Law Society of America, San Diego, California, October 6–9, 1975* (Washington, DC: CLSA, 1976), 26–37.

5. Gerhard Ludwig Müller, "Divorced and Remarried," *L'Osservatore Romano* (October 23, 2013), Eng. trans. Vatican Radio at Zenit.org (October 24, 2013).

6. "Recent Proposals for the Pastoral Care of the Divorced and Remarried: A Theological Assessment," Eng. ed., *Nova et Vetera* 12 (2014): 601–30.

7. Synod 14, *Relatio Synodi* of the III Extraordinary General Assembly of the Synod of Bishops: "Pastoral Challenges to the Family in the Context of Evangelization" (October 5–19, 2014), Press Office Bulletin 10/18/14 (Vatican City State: Sala Stampa della Santa Sede, 2014), 3, http://press.vatican.va/content/sala stampa/en/bollettino/pubblico/2014/10/18/0770.html, hereafter cited as *Relatio Synodi*.

8. *Relatio Synodi* 12.

9. *Relatio Synodi* 13.

10. Report at Zenit.org (May 7, 2014) of an interview of Cardinal Baldisseri in the Christian weekly magazine *Tertio*, http://www.zenit.org/en/articles/cardinal-church-needs-to-update-doctrine-on-marriage.

11. Edward Schillebeeckx, *Marriage: Human Reality and Saving Mystery*, trans. N. D. Smith (New York: Sheed & Ward, 1965), 392.

12. Karl Rahner, *Theological Investigations*, vol. 10 (Baltimore: Helicon Press, 1973), 199.

13. Robert Imbelli, "Family in Focus," *America* 211, no. 18 (December 8, 2014), 21.

14. Schillebeeckx, *Marriage*, 142–43.

15. Theodore Mackin, *Divorce and Remarriage* (New York: Paulist Press, 1984), 91–93.

16. John Meier, *A Marginal Jew: Rethinking the Historical Jesus*, vol. 4 (New Haven & London: Yale University Press, 2009), 118.

17. Raymond F. Collins, *Divorce in the New Testament* (Collegeville, MI: The Liturgical Press, 1992), 214–15.

18. Denziger-Schönmetzer, *Enchiridion Symbolorum Definitionum et Declarationum De Rebus Fidei et Morum, Decretum de sacramento matrimonii*, Can. 7, (Freiberg: Herder, 1963), 416, no. 1807.

19. Denziger-Schönmetzer, *Decretum de sacramentis in genere*, Can. 1, no. 1601, 382. See also *Decretum de sacramento matrimonii*, Can. 1, 416, no. 1801.

20. Denziger-Schönmetzer, *Decretum de sacramentis in genere*, Can. 2, 382, no. 1602.

21. See, for example, *coram* Pompedda, May 9, 1970, *Decisiones Sacrae Romanae Rotae* 62 (1970): 476; *coram* Pasquazi, July 28, 1960, *Decisiones* 53 (1961): 429; *coram* Masala, November 20, 1969, *Decisiones* 61 (1969): 1034.

22. Pontifical Commission for the Revision of the Code of Canon Law, *Communicationes* 15 (1983): 231.

23. Ibid., 9 (1977): 374–75; 15 (1983): 233–34.

24. Ibid., 15 (1983): 233.

25. Pope Benedict XVI, Apostolic Letter *motu proprio*, "Omnium in mentem" (October 26, 2009).

26. Richard Malone and John R. Connery, eds., *Contemporary Perspectives on Christian Marriage: Propositions and Papers from the International Theological Commission* (Chicago: Loyola University Press, 1984), 3–36, hereafter cited as *ITC*.

27. Jan Grootaers and Joseph Selling, *The 1980 Synod of Bishops "On the Role of the Family": An Exposition of the Event and An Analysis of its Texts* (Leuven: Leuven University Press, 1983), 270, no. 145.

28. Pope John Paul II, "The Natural Dimension of Marriage," *Origins* 30, no. 36 (February 22, 2001): 583, no. 8.

29. Pope Benedict XVI, "Address of His Holiness Benedict XVI for the Inauguration of the Judicial Year of the Tribunal of the Roman Rota," January 26, 2013 (Rome: Libreria Editrice Vaticana, 2013).

30. See, for example, the two decisions *coram Serrano* published in *Sacramentalità e Validità del Matrimonio nella Giurisprudenza del Tribunale della Rota Romana* (Città del Vaticano: Libreria Editrice Vaticana, 1995): *Romana* (April 18, 1986), 203–15; *Compobassen* (June 1, 1990), 269–84. See also Serrano's own work, *Ispirazione conciliare nei principi generali del matrimonio canonico* (Bologna, 1985), 43–44.

31. *Coram* Boccafola (P.N. 19.526, June 25, 2009; unpublished, translated by author) nos. 6–7; see also M. Pompedda, "Fede e sacramento del matrimonio," *Quaderni Studio Rotale II* (Rome, 1987), 450.

32. *Coram Sciacca* (June 1, 2007), no. 13.

33. *Relatio Synodi* 14.

34. *ITC* 4.4.

35. Cf. especially C. 27, 2 of the *Decretum Gratiani*.

36. Petrus Lombardus, *Libri IV Sententiarum*, 2nd ed. (Ad Claras Aquas: Patres Collegii S. Bonaventurae, 1916), l. IV, d. 27, cap. 2, 3, 4.

37. Cf. C. 27, 2, d. p. c. 39 of the *Decretum Gratiani*.

38. James Coriden, *The Indissolubility Added to Christian Marriage by Consummation* (Rome: Catholic Book Agency, 1961), 26.

39. "…un certain manque d'équilibre qui se fera sentir dans toute la suite du temps." A. Esmein et al., *Le mariage en droit canonique*, 12th ed., vol. 1 (Paris: Recueil Sirey, 1935), 139.

40. See Jean Mouroux, *The Meaning of Man* (Garden City: Doubleday/Image Books, 1961), passim.

41. James A. Brundage, *Law, Sex, and Christian Society in Medieval Europe* (Chicago/London: The University of Chicago Press, 1987), 136.

42. Ibid., 128–29.

43. See canon 1057 §2 of the current Code in comparison to its predecessor, CIC 1081 §2, in the 1917 Code.

44. *Relatio Synodi* 48.

45. John T. Noonan Jr., *Power to Dissolve: Lawyers and Marriages in the Courts of the Roman Curia* (Cambridge, MA: The Belknap Press of Harvard University Press, 1972), 136.

46. *Communicationes* 10 (1978): 108.

Part Two:
Streamlining Canon Law

In light of the reflections of Part One on the meaning of sacramental marriage, there are many improvements to be considered in the area of both *substantive and procedural law*, a need experienced by tribunal personnel for decades. It is a need that was not fully addressed by the 1983 revision of the Code of Canon Law, despite the fifth principle of revision on subsidiarity, summarized as follows:

> Procedural law should be uniform throughout the universal Church but can be given a more general and universal form, leaving to regional authorities the faculty to enact rules to be observed in their respective tribunals.[1]

Canon law in this area, including the instruction *Dignitas Connubii*, is universal to the point of stultifying uniformity. This need was articulated in the Synod deliberations although suggestions for improvement remained somewhat general. Moreover, prior to the beginning of the Synod, Pope Francis already established a separate papal commission, chaired by Msgr. Pio Vito Pinto, dean of the Roman Rota, to simplify and streamline canonical procedure while safeguarding the principle of the indissolubility of matrimony.[2]

Most needed is a procedure crafted specifically for matrimonial cases, rather than an amendment of existing norms. The process to handle matrimonial cases should be *ecclesiastical* in the best sense of the term. The procedures should neither imitate civil law nor strive to be juridical in an abstract or academic sense. The sole *dubium* to be addressed should be whether the marriage is, within the meaning of the Church's doctrine and law, invalid from the beginning and, with an expanded concept of consummation, whether the marriage in question, if it was valid or at least presumably valid, was ever completed, that is, ever became absolutely indissoluble as Christ commanded.

Accordingly, this procedure should not be a species of the ordinary contentious process, which although improved by the 1983 Code, is still cumbersome, unnecessary, and, generally speaking, inappropriate.[3] The process must begin from the fact that marriage is uniquely sacred and sometimes sacramental. In such an inquiry, any "contentious" party-v.-party dynamic is invariably about issues that have nothing to do with validity and indissolubility. *Dignitas Connubii* Art. 102 improved the situation somewhat when it recognized the fact that, in certain cases, the spouses need not be "opposing" parties. In their commentary on this canon, Lüdicke and Jenkins note, "This reasonable norm recognizes that the spouses as parties to the process...play a different role than they would in an ordinary contentious trial."[4]

When parties demonstrate real opposition to each other in a tribunal process it is usually about who "wins" rather than about the Church's determination of nullity. The tribunal should not be an enabler of such antagonism nor should its procedure appear in any way similar to what has often occurred between the parties in a secular divorce proceeding. Instead, the tribunal should follow a theologically and canonically nuanced and pastoral process that allows the judge simply to examine the concrete facts and make a judgment about freedom to marry within the meaning of Church teaching. In the same vein, a defender of the bond should be required solely in cases where the case is decided by a single judge not to provide an artificial form of "contentious process" but simply to facilitate a reasonable discussion prior to the final determination.

For centuries, controversies and questions were adjudicated in very informal and local synodal gatherings and by bishops with the help of canonical advisers (somewhat like the "administrative means under the jurisdiction of the diocesan bishop" proposed at the Synod).[5] Over seven centuries ago, in a decree titled *Dispendiosam*, promulgated at the Council of Vienne (1311–12), Clement V approved a "streamlined" procedure called by Italian jurists "the summary process," which was applicable in almost all cases, including marriage cases. The following from the decree *Saepe Contingit* gives the flavor of how flexible the Clementine process was:

> In some of those cases we order those courts to proceed simply and easily and without the pomp and circumstance of a judicial proceeding….a judge to whom we commit cases of this kind: need not necessarily demand a formal libellus or a joinder of issues;…may shorten deadlines; may…shorten the trial by denying exceptions and dilatory and unnecessary appeals, and by restricting the contentions and disputes of the parties, advocates and procurators, and by limiting the number of witnesses. A judge may not, however, abbreviate a trial by curtailing necessary proofs or legitimate defenses. Lest the truth remain concealed…neither the citation nor the taking of the usual oaths of good faith and intent and to tell the truth may ever be omitted.

The 1917 Code merged the summary and ordinary contentious procedures into a new procedure that was the worst of both worlds, at least for marriage cases. The Instruction *Provida Mater Ecclesia* nineteen years later tried to tailor the process to marriage cases since, as the document underwhelmingly states in its Introduction, "the judges of diocesan curiae…sometimes encounter many difficulties."[6]

The *American Procedural Norms* in 1970 and Paul VI's *Causas Matrimoniales* the following year made changes that certainly facilitated marriage proceedings, and most of these were incorporated systematically into the 1983 Code. Nonetheless, there was still a felt need for tailoring the matrimonial process, which led to the interdicasterial Instruction *Dignitas Connubii* twenty-two years later (paralleling what happened with the first Code). As helpful as certain norms of *Dignitas Connubii* have been for tribunal personnel, the Instruction does little more than did *Provida* for the prior Code, namely, offer "a coordinated restatement of the ruling of the Code on matrimonial procedure."[7]

The following represents a list of specific canonical changes that might serve as the basis for a truly "matrimonial" procedure, a procedure that, while remaining objective and official, would be essentially pastoral and sacramental.

A. SUBSTANTIVE MARRIAGE LAW

The Code of Canon Law cannot *resolve* current theological debates; this must be done by the Magisterium. But, in the same vein, it should not retain as juridical elements propositions that *hinder* theological development. Accordingly, the following recommendations should be given consideration:

1. Canon 1055 (the conciliar description of marriage): Taken almost word-for-word from *Gaudium et Spes*, no. 48, paragraph 1 reads as follows:

The matrimonial covenant, by which a man and a woman establish between themselves a partnership of the whole of life and which is ordered by its nature to the good of the spouses and the procreation and education of offspring, has been raised by Christ the Lord to the dignity of a sacrament between the baptized.

This very first paragraph of the marriage canons highlights the personalist nature of the object of marriage, the persons themselves, and purposely refrains from repeating the hierarchy of ends found in c. 1013 §1 of the 1917 Code.

Paragraph 2, however, represents an unfortunate juxtaposition of canon 1012 §2 of the 1917 Code with the conciliar description:

For this reason, a valid matrimonial contract cannot exist between the baptized without it being by that fact a sacrament.

Paragraph 2 should be deleted. The reference to the dignity of the sacrament in paragraph 1 and the "special firmness" of the properties of unity and indissolubility of a sacramental marriage mentioned later in canon 1056 are sufficient to connect the baptism of the spouses and marital sacramentality. This change would also remove one of the few paragraphs in which marriage is referred to as a "contract" rather than a "covenant."

2. *Canon 1061 (consummation):* Paragraph 1 should be simplified in order to leave the area of consummation room to develop. It should read,

A valid marriage between the baptized is called *ratum tantum* if it has not been consummated; it is called *ratum et consummatum* if it has been consummated.

The canon goes on to define the juridical elements of physical "consummation" as follows:

...if the spouses have performed between themselves in a human fashion a conjugal act which is suitable in itself for the procreation of offspring, to which marriage is ordered by its nature and by which the spouses become one flesh.

This description should be deleted, leaving room to interpret the notion of consummation as more than a single physical marital act. This would also solve the canon's failure to include "good of the spouses" as an end of marriage (as stated in c. 1055 §1) and would, at the same time, remove the inaccurate use of the scriptural phrase "*una caro*" as referring to the physical act rather than to the entire interpersonal union of the couple. If paragraph 1 is amended in this way, then paragraphs two and three on the presumption of consummation and putative marriage could remain.

§2. After a marriage has been celebrated, if the spouses have lived together consummation is presumed until the contrary is proven.

§3. An invalid marriage is called putative if at least one party celebrated it in good faith, until both parties become certain of its nullity.

3. **Canons 1058, 1085 §2, 1098, 1101 §2 (contract v. covenant):** Greater consistency of thought can be achieved concerning marriage as "covenant" (the important description of *Gaudium et Spes* and canon 1055 §1) by changing the phrase "*contract marriage*" to "*enter the covenant of marriage*" or "*celebrate marriage*" in these canons and any others where it appears.

4. **Canon 1101 §2 (invalidating intentions):** The phrase "the sacramental dignity of marriage" should be added to paragraph 2 in order to clarify the fact that, when both parties are baptized, either would invalidate his or her consent by specifically excluding sacramentality. The revised canon would then read,

> §2. If, however, either or both parties by a positive act of the will exclude marriage itself, **the sacramental dignity of marriage,** some essential element of marriage, or some essential property of marriage, the party **enters the covenant of marriage** invalidly.

5. **Canon 1102 (conditional consent):** As in canon 826 of the *Code for the Eastern Churches,* no marriage should be permitted if consent is in any way conditioned; such consent is incongruous with the personalist understanding of marriage flowing from *Gaudium et Spes* and canon 1055 §1. The three paragraphs of canon 1102 should be replaced by the simple statement found in canon 826 of the code for the Eastern Churches, which also has the advantage of avoiding use of the word *contract*, replacing it with *celebrate*: **Marriage based on a condition cannot be validly celebrated.**

6. **Canon 1142 (*dissolution of nonconsummated marriages*)** **and canons 1141–50 in general.** Canon 1142 reads as follows:

> For a just cause, the Roman Pontiff can dissolve a non-consummated marriage between baptized persons or between a baptized party and a non-baptized party at the request of both parties or of one of them, even if the other party is unwilling.

> "Roman Pontiff" should be replaced with "diocesan bishop." Diocesan bishops should be authorized to dissolve all marriages that are not absolutely indissoluble—both the nonconsummated marriages of canon 1142 and marriages that are not sacramental insofar as at least one of the spouses is not baptized, that is, dissolutions "in favor of the faith." This entire area of dissolution is a part of marriage law that could be responsibly decentralized, making the process more personal, pastoral, efficient—in other words, "streamlined."

As the Church's understanding about the sacramentality and indissolubility of marriage develops, all the canons on marriage must be reviewed and, where required, amended. The above six suggestions, however, could be accomplished immediately in order to keep the wording of the canons an accurate reflection of our current understanding of marriage and, at the same time, leave the canons open to the mystery of the sacrament which Jesus revealed to us.

B. PROCEDURAL MARRIAGE LAW

1. **Contentious process:** One of the most fundamental problems with matrimonial procedure for declarations of

invalidity is the placement of the process within the category of "contentious cases," that is, cases in which a plaintiff sues a defendant. Canon 1691 currently requires the use of the canons on trials in general and on the ordinary contentious trial to be applied to marriage cases. This requirement should be abrogated. As Msgr. Lawrence Wrenn stated so clearly in a 1986 article titled "A Balanced Procedural Law,"

> the problem is that the whole tone of a contentious process is wrong for a marriage case, especially an open-and-shut one that is completely uncontested, and all the tinkering in the world is not going to correct that problem. True balance is never achieved that way.[8]

Actually, the idea of drafting a unique process rather than simply a few special matrimonial canons had been considered by the Code Commission during the pre-1983 revision process but without success. In the end, the drafting committee chose to stay with the procedural format of the 1917 Code, which was very unfortunate.[9]

The time has come to develop a completely unique matrimonial process to replace canons 1671–91. The new process need not be universal in every detail; local circumstances should prevail in certain areas. Episcopal conferences should be commissioned to concretize tribunal practice for their people and in accordance with their ecclesiastical resources. This is what should have happened in the 1983 Code and in *Dignitas Connubii*. It should be required now.

2. **The right of defense:** A person who begins a marriage case is called a "petitioner" or "plaintiff," the other party a "respondent" or "defendant." Much is made of the respondent's "right of defense." This major emphasis in jurisprudence is a subset of the requirement that marriage cases be treated as a contentious trial. A respondent, however, who refuses to cooperate out of spite in order to deprive the petitioner of the sacraments should have few if any rights. Any "right of defense" should simply be: (a) the defense by all concerned of the *Church's teaching* about marriage; (b) the defense of the *right of all persons to marry* if they are not prohibited by law; (c) the defense of the right of the parties, motivated solely by their desire for reconciliation with the Church, to have the opportunity to *present their perspective* on their marriage to the tribunal and to receive a *speedy, just, and merciful resolution* of their pastoral situation.

3. **The defender of the bond:** Currently, the defender of the bond must intervene in every marriage case. This is an outmoded juridical device. The defender of the bond should not be required to argue for the bond but solely *pro rei veritate*, for the truth of the matter. His or her task should be to assist the judge in making an authentic decision about the right to marry on the part of the two parties in light of Church teaching. In a sense, the roles of defender (cc. 1432–36; *DC* 52–56 & 59–60) and assessor (c. 1424 and *DC* 52) should be merged to provide a single aide to the judge (a role in many secular legal systems carried out by the judge's "clerk").

4. **Changing the grounds:** In marriage cases, a judge should have the flexibility to change the ground of nullity (or failure to consummate) at appropriate points in the process

whenever the evidence supports it. (Currently, canon 1514 makes such a change invalid unless it is established "by a new decree, for a grave cause, at the request of a party, and after the other parties have been heard and their arguments considered.")

5. ***The Roman Rota:*** The Rota has been a champion of refining marriage law. (For example, today there would be no canon 1095, 2°&3° on lack of discretion of judgment and the incapacity to assume the essential obligations of marriage without the Rotal decisions that long preceded its formulation.) It is counterproductive, however, for Rotal judges to be embroiled in cases of second instance, often enough brought to them simply because a disgruntled respondent has the resources to appeal directly to the Rota in Rome, usually as a malicious device to delay resolution of the petitioner's pastoral situation. The Rota should, instead, act as a supreme court, judging only third-instance cases that involve conflicting sentences in the lower tribunals in order to give sound guidance on deep-seated theological and canonical issues. In unusual circumstances, there could be a procedure similar to a writ of certiorari in civil law by which the Rota could order a particular case to be remanded to itself or for the Signatura to arrange such a referral to the Rota.

6. ***Competence:*** Canon 1673, 3º allows a matrimonial case to be heard, under certain conditions, in the petitioner's diocese of domicile:

> 3° …provided that both parties live in the territory of the same conference of bishops and the judicial vicar of the domicile of the respondent gives consent after he has heard the respondent.

These conditions are unduly restrictive. To give a typical example: a marriage in which the petitioner lives in New York City and his or her ex-spouse lives in Puerto Rico cannot use this forum unless the Apostolic Signatura in Rome grants special permission. (Puerto Rico is not part of the United States Conference of Catholic Bishops.)

The canon should be revised to declare the tribunal of the petitioner's stable residence (rather than canonical domicile) to be an ordinary forum without the need for special permissions. This would respect the fact that a matrimonial case is not a dispute between parties about whether to remain together or not. It would reinforce the central purpose of the procedure: to decide about the petitioner's (and often the respondent's) request to marry someone else "in the Lord," to achieve reconciliation with God and the Church and to allow Catholics in second marriages to regularize their situations and participate in the mystery of the Eucharist.

7. **Single judge:** Matrimonial cases should ordinarily be judged by a single qualified judge with a defender/assessor; if judged by a collegiate tribunal, the intervention of the defender/assessor should be optional insofar as the three judges provide sufficient consultation and discussion, not to mention judicial voting.

8. **Lay judges:** The role of single judge should not be limited to priests and deacons. Laymen and women who are qualified should be able to serve as a single judge instead of being restricted, as they are now by canon 1421 §2, to collegiate tribunals, or serving solely as assessors (who end up in some cases being ghostwriters). Training and expertise and the recognition of such qualifications by an episcopal

appointment are what matter, not whether one happens to be a member of the clerical state.

9. ***Appeals:*** Appeal of a first instance affirmative decision by the defender/assessor should be optional and based on weighty reasons. If the defender/assessor sees no reason to appeal, he should state in writing that not even an appellate review is needed and the judgment should then be executed. If the defender/assessor is of the opinion that the judgment should be reviewed at the appellate level, he should state this rationale in writing for the benefit of the second instance review.

10. ***Review at the second level:***

   a. ***Review:*** The current review process for affirmative first instance sentences wastes resources by requiring an appellate defender and a college of three judges in order to issue a simple confirmatory decree of an affirmative sentence (c. 1682 §2). Any review and the ensuing decree should be in the hands of a single judge, lay or cleric, taking into consideration the first instance animadversions of the defender/assessor who has called for the review and/or any dissenting judicial opinion in a collegiate tribunal (c. 1609 §4), as well as the declarations and reasoning of the parties. The appellate defender/assessor should have the option of offering animadversions prior to completion of the review to assist in situating all such final decisions within the context of the Church's teaching on marriage.

   b. ***The Acts:*** When an appellate tribunal reviews a marriage case, it normally does not need to see the entire record, with all the evidence. The first instance tribunal should be required to send simply the Acts that were specified in *Causas Matrimoniales* VIII, 2: the sentence; the animadversions of the first instance defender; the observations, if any, of the parties. The appellate tribunal can always demand additional information in individual cases if needed for its review.

11. ***Appellate trials:*** If the original sentence is not confirmed by the initial appellate review but is, instead, remanded to an appellate trial, the same rules should exist at second instance for the constitution of the tribunal: a single judge with a defender/assessor or a collegiate tribunal with an optional defender/assessor.

NOTES

1. John A. Alesandro, "General Introduction," in *The Code of Canon Law: A Text and Commentary*, ed. James A. Coriden et al. (New York: Paulist Press, 1985), 6.

2. 2014-09-21 Vatican Radio, News.va, Official Vatican Network.

3. Canon 1691: "In other procedural matters, the canons on trials in general and on the ordinary contentious trial must be applied unless the nature of the matter precludes it; the special norms for cases concerning the status of persons and cases pertaining to the public good are to be observed."

4. Klaus Lüdicke and Ronny Jenkins, Dignitas Connubii: *Norms and Commentary* (Washington, DC: Canon Law Society of America, 2006), 183–84.

5. *Relatio Synodi* 48.

6. S.C. for the Sacraments, Instruction *Provida Mater Ecclesia*, *AAS* 28 (1936): 313 in T. Bouscaren, ed. *Canon Law Digest*, vol. 2 (Milwaukee: Bruce, 1956), 471.

7. William Doheny, commenting on *Provida: Canonical Procedure in Matrimonial Cases: Formal Judicial Procedure* (Milwaukee: Bruce, 1938), 3.

8. Lawrence A. Wrenn, "A Balanced Procedural Law," *The Jurist* 46 (1986): 621.

9. *Communicationes* 6 (1974): 39–41; 10 (1978): 209–12.

Conclusions

In summary, the Church's canonical construct of marriage and the procedure for applying it both need radical surgery. We are losing the battle for marriage as a sacrament of the new covenant both in the parish and in the tribunal. In general, the frequency of marriage has declined, a phenomenon reflected in Church practice. Far fewer couples are approaching the Church to be married before a priest or deacon. Over the past twenty-five years, there has been a 52 percent decrease in the number of Catholic marriages in the United States in contrast to a 30 percent increase in the Catholic population (which tracks closely the overall increase in U.S. population of 29 percent). According to the statistics published by *The Official Catholic Directory* for the years in question, 341,622 Catholic marriages were celebrated in 1988 whereas, in 2013, only 163,976 took place.

At the same time, divorce continues to be a major concern for all, including Catholics. While many divorced Catholics may fortunately be able to receive a declaration of freedom to marry because they never married in Church to begin with, there are thousands of Catholics every year who, though divorced, are still bound to a presumably valid marriage or Catholics entering a marriage for the first time who are desirous of marrying a baptized non-Catholic who is similarly bound by a sacramental marriage according to Church teaching.

And yet, even though, as then-Archbishop Müller opined, "marriages nowadays are probably invalid more often than they were previously,"[1] the number of cases being adjudicated by Catholic tribunals in the United States has, in the last quarter of a century, dropped drastically, perhaps by half. A sampling by the author of thirteen representative tribunals in the United States (large and small and geographically diverse) based on figures collected by the Canon Law Society of America over a twenty-five-year period ending in 2013, offered startling results. Every one of the thirteen tribunals issued fewer formal decisions about marriage nullity: the smallest reduction was 17 percent, the largest 88 percent; ten of the thirteen tribunals were above 50 percent. The formal decisions about nullity by these thirteen tribunals totaled 6,942 in 1988 while in 2013 they amounted to only 2,170, a decrease of 4,772 (69 percent). Couples are voting with their feet.

The sacrament of marriage has been given by Christ to his Church to build up the people of God not merely by procreating children but by fostering Christian families in their ministry of living a life of love for God and one another. This sacrificial life should be marked not only by the cross but by daily resurrection to new life. It should be life-giving and life-affirming.

For too long, the Church has unnecessarily juridicized marriage, downplaying its truly sacred and, in many cases, sacramental character and reducing it to the secular. It is time to liberate the sacrament of marriage from its austere identification with natural marriage by recognizing its sacramental uniqueness and, at the same time, to free our tribunals from slavish imitation of civil law by providing them with a truly ecclesial process to examine marriages that have broken down.

The revision of canon law cannot on its own turn things around, but it can help. The Code should be purged of whatever norms are inconsistent with the sacrament; and at the same time, jurisprudence should be empowered to rediscover the newness of Christ in today's marital experiences.

- The sacrament of marriage should be a celebration of faith and judged as such.
- The sacrament of marriage should be recognized not as a natural marriage of two persons who happen to be baptized but as a deep interpersonal encounter of faith, as mysterious as that of Christ's incarnation, one that over time (a time that may be unique for each couple) becomes indissoluble in the best sense of our Christian tradition and the teaching of Christ in the Gospels.
- Procedures for helping those in failed marriages should be sacramental (rather than secular) in character and pastoral in application (rather than juridical).
- We should stop worrying about how many declarations of nullity are granted, based on invalid consent, and turn our attention and concern to how few Catholics we are helping to be reconciled with the people of God and to enjoy being fully active members of the Body of Christ.

In promulgating the 1983 Code, Pope John Paul II stated that the purpose of canon law is "to create such an order in ecclesial society that, while assigning the *primacy to love, grace and charisms*, it at the same time renders their organic development easier in the life of both the ecclesial society and the individual persons who belong to it."[2] It is quite a challenge to combine God's revealed mercy and love with a legal process. The legal may keep things orderly and clear, but it may also have the unfortunate effect of confining the love and reducing the Divine to the purely human. This is what has happened with Christian marriage.

It is the Church's obligation in every age to return to the source, Jesus Christ, and renew his meaning in the context of contemporary challenges. As Pope Francis put it on October 4, 2014, in his address at the Vigil of Prayer preceding the opening of the Synod,

> Is not the history of the Church recounted perhaps with many similar situations, that our fathers were able to overcome with obstinate patience and creativity? The secret is in a look: …to maintain our gaze fixed on Jesus Christ.…If we assume His way of thinking, of living and of relating to others, we will not tire of translating the Synodal works into guidelines and courses for the pastoral on the person and on the family.[3]

The pastoral challenges the Church is facing in regard to marriage are staggering. They have emerged, however, not simply from the practicalities of modern life but from a fundamental reductionism in regard to the teaching of Christ that has juridicized the sacrament over the centuries. As the Synod of Bishops conducts its assembly in October 2015 and follows up on it, the updating of our Church's canonical construct in the areas of sacramentality, indissolubility, and consummation must be addressed at the deepest level. If this task is beyond the scope of this Synod, then it must be addressed by some other form of authentic teaching so that practical solutions will be authentic applications of these underlying scriptural, doctrinal, and theological principles.

If canonical equity and the principle of *salus animarum* teach us anything, it is that the juridical must *facilitate* the gospel and the pastoral life of the faithful. Human law is at the service of and must cede to divine law, not vice versa; "love, grace and charisms" remain *primary*.

That is, of course, what, over four hundred years ago, Shakespeare had Portia argue in Venice:

The quality of mercy is not strain'd,
It droppeth as the gentle rain from heaven
Upon the place beneath: it is twice blest;
It blesseth him that gives and him that takes.

It may be that we have too rigidly "strain'd" Jesus' gentle gift from heaven, the sacrament of matrimony. Let it be our happy task, with Pope Francis's "obstinate patience," to release it in every way possible so that we may see it flower as Christ intended for his new covenant. Then marriage will not simply be its "old" self, but will be, as God has designed it for the new covenant of grace, truly "new."

Msgr. John A. Alesandro, JCD, JD

NOTES

1. Müller, "Divorced and Remarried."

2. Pope John Paul II, "Sacrae disciplinae leges," *Code of Canon Law: Latin-English Edition, New English Translation* (Washington, DC: CLSA, 2012), xxix–xxx (emphasis added).

3. Pope Francis, "Discourse at Vigil of Prayer for the Synod on the Family, http://www.zenit.org/en/articles/pope-francis-discourse-at-vigil-of-prayer-for-the-synod-on-the-family.